TRIBES of NATIVE AMERICA

Cheyenne

edited by Marla Felkins Ryan
and Linda Schmittroth

BLACKBIRCH®
PRESS

J 978.004 CHEYENNE CHE
Cheyenne
31994013675100

THOMSON
———★———™
GALE

San Diego • Detroit • New York • San Francisco • Cleveland
New Haven, Conn. • Waterville, Maine • London • Munich

LIBRARY OF CONGRESS CATALOGING-IN-PUBLICATION DATA

Cheyenne / Marla Felkins Ryan, book editor; Linda Schmittroth, book editor.
   v. cm. — (Tribes of Native America)
Includes bibliographical references and index.
Contents: Name — Origins and group affiliations — The Sand Creek Massacre —
Language — Economy — Daily life — Customs — Current tribal issues.
  ISBN 1-56711-606-X (alk. paper)
1. Cheyenne Indians—Juvenile literature. [1. Cheyenne Indians. 2. Indians of North
America—Great Plains.] I. Ryan, Marla Felkins. II. Schmittroth, Linda. III. Series.
  E99.C53 C53 2003
  978.004'973—dc21   2002008668

Printed in United States
10 9 8 7 6 5 4 3 2 1

Table of Contents

CHEYENNE

Name

The Cheyenne (*shy-ANN*) called themselves *Tsistsistas*.
It meant "beautiful people" or "our people." The name
Cheyenne comes from the Sioux word *shyela*. It means
"red talkers" or "people of different speech."

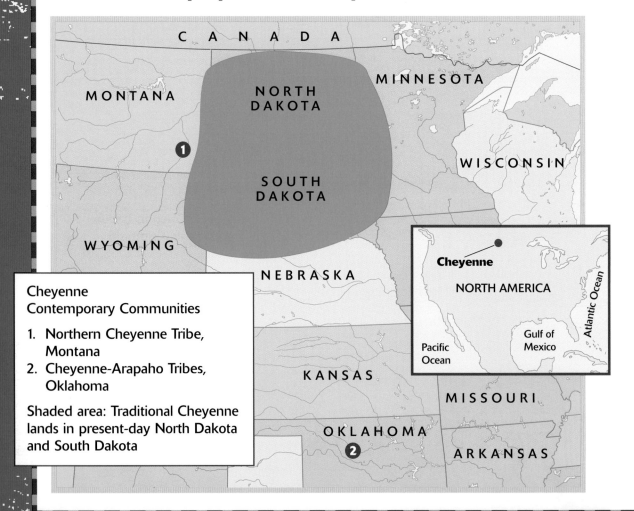

Cheyenne
Contemporary Communities

1. Northern Cheyenne Tribe,
   Montana
2. Cheyenne-Arapaho Tribes,
   Oklahoma

Shaded area: Traditional Cheyenne
lands in present-day North Dakota
and South Dakota

Where are the traditional Cheyenne lands?

Most Cheyenne live on the Great Plains. They live mainly in Montana, South Dakota, and Oklahoma.

Cheyenne men in traditional war paint and clothing

What has happened to the population?

No one is sure how many Cheyenne there were in the past. Around 3,500 Cheyenne may have lived on the Great Plains in 1800. In a 1990 population count by the U.S. Bureau of the Census, 7,104 people said they were Cheyenne.

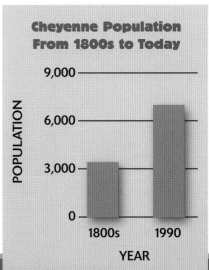

Cheyenne Population From 1800s to Today

POPULATION	

9,000

6,000

3,000

0

1800s   1990

YEAR

Origins and group ties

The Cheyenne once lived near the Great Lakes. They were forced to move west by other eastern tribes. In the Great Plains, the Cheyenne united with the Sutaio tribe. The Sutaio had also been forced from their Great Lakes home. In the 1990s, one main group of Cheyenne lived on the Northern Cheyenne Reservation in Montana. The other main group lived on the Cheyenne-Arapaho Reservation in Oklahoma.

The story of the Cheyenne is one of movement. They were forced to move westward by their constant search for food. Other tribes also pushed them west. These tribes were also forced west as the white population grew. The Cheyenne had one of the most highly organized native governments. They were also famous for their mighty warriors and their spiritual ways.

In the 1800s, many Cheyenne left their villages to follow buffalo herds.

The Cheyenne lived near the Great Lakes until they were forced to move west by other tribes.

HISTORY

The move west

The Cheyenne probably came from the western Great Lakes region of what is now Minnesota. In the early 1600s, they began to meet French and English fur traders. The first Europeans to see them were probably the French explorers who built Fort Crevecoeur on the Illinois River. The Cheyenne lived nearby in farming communities. During the late 1600s, the Cheyenne moved to present-day North and South Dakota. There, they built villages of earthen dwellings and farmed the land.

After the Cheyenne acquired horses, they adopted a wandering lifestyle.

White settlers traveled through Cheyenne territory as they moved west across the Great Plains.

In time, pressure from the Sioux and Ojibway tribes drove the Cheyenne even farther west, to the Black Hills. By the 1800s, the Cheyenne had horses. They could then hunt for food on horseback. Many left their villages to follow the buffalo across the Great Plains. In the first quarter of the 19th century, the tribe split into two groups. The Northern Cheyenne roamed the northern country in search of horses and buffalo. The Southern Cheyenne made a permanent home along the Arkansas River in Colorado.

Conflict

During the mid-19th century, the Cheyenne faced great changes. The United States took much of the land in the West. White settlers streamed westward. They traveled on trails that passed through the land of the Cheyenne and other

1876
The Northern Cheyenne join the Sioux to defeat Lieutenant Colonel George Custer at the Battle of the Little Bighorn

1884
The Northern Cheyenne Reservation is set up in eastern Montana

1917–1918
WWI fought in Europe

1929
Stock market crash begins the Great Depression

1941
Bombing at Pearl Harbor forces United States into WWII

1950s
Reservations no longer controlled by federal government

1989–1990
The National Museum of the American Indian Act and the Native American Grave Protection and Reparations Act bring about the return of burial remains to native tribes

tribes. The growing white population quickly reduced the number of buffalo. As a result, armed fights between the Indians and whites grew more and more common. The U.S. government tried to protect white settlers. It also gave money to the tribes to help pay for the lost buffalo and land.

The Sand Creek Massacre

In 1851, the U.S. government and 11 tribes, including the Cheyenne, signed the Treaty of Fort Laramie. It said that the U.S. government would give payments to the Great Plains Indians each year. It also set the

In 1851, the Cheyenne and 10 other tribes signed a peace treaty at Fort Laramie, Wyoming (pictured).

borders of the land owned by each tribe. In return, the Indians agreed that the United States could build roads and military posts on their lands. They also agreed to end tribal warfare and to stop their attacks on white settlers. By 1856, though, tensions rose again. The number of whites who crossed the Indians' land continued to grow. From 1857 to 1879, a war was fought between the Cheyenne and the U.S. Army. The bloodiest event of that war was the Sand Creek Massacre.

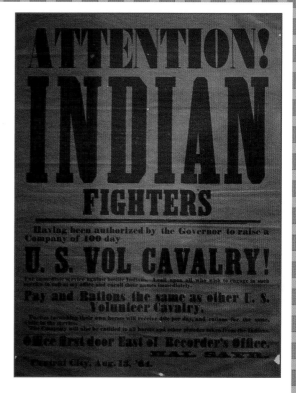

The U.S. Army used posters like this one to call for volunteers to fight Indians.

Southern Cheyenne Chief Black Kettle had tried to make peace between his people and the government. In 1861, he signed a treaty that gave up all Cheyenne lands to the United States. The Cheyenne kept only the small Sand Creek Reservation in southern Colorado. This barren land could not support the people. In time, many young Cheyenne men decided that to survive, they had to steal the livestock and goods of nearby white settlers. One of their raids made whites very angry. The settlers then sent an armed force that opened fire on the first group of Cheyenne it met.

Whites killed more than 100 Cheyenne people during the Sand Creek Massacre in 1884.

Black Kettle spoke with the local military commander. He was told that he and his people would be safe if they stayed at the Sand Creek Reservation. Black Kettle was betrayed, however. On November 29, 1884, a large group of Cheyenne and Arapaho were asleep at Sand Creek. Colonel John M. Chivington and his Colorado Volunteers came in and slaughtered 105 women and children and 28 men. Black Kettle rode into the gunfire. He waved his American flag to show that he was under the protection of the U.S. government. It was no use. The Indians' settlement was destroyed by fire. Their horses were scattered across the plains. After the massacre, the U.S. Congress held hearings. The government formally criticized the event and the men who were in charge of it.

Custer's defeat

The Medicine Lodge Treaty of 1867 set up a reservation for the Southern Cheyenne and Arapaho in northern Oklahoma. The Northern Cheyenne continued to fight the Americans. The conflict peaked with the 1876 Battle of the Little Bighorn. In that battle, the tribe helped the Sioux defeat Lieutenant Colonel George Armstrong Custer (1839–1876). In response, U.S. troops rounded up the Northern Cheyenne who took part in the battle. They were forced to move to the reservation in Oklahoma. The people missed their northern homeland. They found

George Armstrong Custer was defeated by Cheyenne and Sioux warriors at the Battle of the Little Bighorn.

After the Battle of the Little Bighorn, Cheyenne people who fought were forced to move to this reservation in Oklahoma.

life on the reservation unbearable. In 1878, they escaped and fled north. American troops caught them in Nebraska. Many died from gunfire and ill treatment by the soldiers. The survivors were sent to Montana. Six years later, in 1884, they were given a small reservation of their own there.

The tribe breaks up

By the 1880s, the buffalo had been hunted to near extinction. The Cheyenne then had to depend on the government for food, shelter, and clothing. State officials in both Oklahoma and Montana tried to encourage the Cheyenne to become ranchers. U.S. officials opposed this, however. They hoped to make the Cheyenne farmers. This plan did not succeed.

Overhunting of buffalo caused the Cheyenne to become dependent on the U.S. government for survival.

In 1887, the Dawes General Allotment Act was passed. It divided reservations into small plots of land, called allotments. These were to be owned and farmed by individual Indians. The rest of the land was opened to white settlement. The breakup of the reservations divided the people and caused Cheyenne culture to break down. Today, the Cheyenne work hard to keep their cultural heritage alive.

Religion

The Cheyenne believed that plants, animals, and people all had spirits. They considered themselves direct descendents

A Cheyenne man prays to the spirit of the earth.

of the creator-god, Heammawihio. This god taught them how to hunt, when to plant and harvest corn, and how to use fire. The Cheyenne prayed to the spirit of the earth. They asked the spirit to make crops grow, to provide herbs, and to heal the sick. They also prayed to the north, south, east, and west. The west, where the sun set and rain and storms began, was the most important of the four directions.

Men prepare for the Sun Dance—the main religious ceremony of the Cheyenne.

The Sun Dance was a common event among many Plains Indians. It was the main religious ceremony of the Cheyenne. It celebrated the power of the sun and tried to renew the earth's resources. The Sun Dance lasted eight days. During the first four days, a dance lodge was built and secret rites were performed in a Lone Tepee. During the last four days, a public dance was held in the Sun Dance Lodge.

In the late 1800s, the U.S. government banned the Sun Dance. The Cheyenne still performed the ceremony, though. They simply renamed it the Willow Dance. In 1911, the Willow Dance was forbidden, too.

Government

Since early times, the Cheyenne have had a highly
organized government. The Council of Forty-Four
was the governing body of the Cheyenne. It met
each year in the summer. It was made up of 44 men
who were elected from 10 Cheyenne groups to serve
10-year terms. Chiefs discussed problems within the
tribe. They also made plans for how to deal with
other tribes. The head of the council, the Sweet

Bundles of grass were sacred objects
in some Cheyenne traditions.

Cheyenne chief Wolf Robe. Many chiefs shared
the responsibility of governing the tribe.

A Cheyenne woman pounds chokecherries. Cheyenne women picked and prepared both berries and roots.

Medicine Chief, had both religious and political duties. He kept the Chief's Medicine, a sacred bundle of grass. He also came up with a code that told how tribal members should behave. The chiefs shared power. There was no one absolute authority.

Today, Montana's Northern Cheyenne tribe is governed by a tribal council. It is made up of a president and 24 council members. Council members from five separate districts are elected to two-year terms. The president serves a four-year term.

Economy

Cheyenne women picked berries and dug up roots that could be eaten. They cooked and dried meat brought home by hunters. They tanned hides, made tepees, and sewed leather clothing and moccasins. Men hunted antelope, buffalo, deer, elk, and wild sheep. They trapped foxes and wolves for their fur.

Northern Cheyenne today work in many jobs. Some work on ranches or for coal companies. Some are firefighters who put out fires throughout the West. Other Cheyenne work in fields such as law and teaching. There are more than 40 small businesses on the reservation. Among them are laundromats, gas stations, grocery stores, and restaurants. The tribe also has a buffalo herd. About 300 Cheyenne serve as social workers and health care workers. Others have jobs in forestry and casinos. The tribe's bingo hall makes about $11,000 a week.

Today, some Cheyenne work as firefighters throughout the West.

The Cheyenne-Arapaho people in Oklahoma earn money from leases on farming and grazing lands, from oil and gas royalties, and from two casinos. Federal funds for Indian tribes have grown smaller over the years. As a result, the Cheyenne have faced problems in their drive to become financially self-sufficient.

DAILY LIFE

Families

When the Cheyenne moved to the Great Plains, they began to use tepees for their homes.

The main duties of the women of the tribe were to care for their homes, raise the children, and gather food. They made furnishings out of grass, earth, and buffalo hides. They also packed belongings when the tribe moved its camps. Men hunted. They also protected the tribe's lands from enemies.

Buildings

The Cheyenne lived as farmers in Minnesota and the eastern Dakotas from the 1600s to the early 1800s. Their homes were lodges made of wooden frames covered with sod. As they moved to the Plains and hunted buffalo, they began to use tepees. These were dwellings made of wooden poles and buffalo hides. They could be moved easily with the help of horses. A fire was built in the center of the tepee. Beds of buffalo robes lined the walls. Men would sometimes paint their tepees with designs they had seen in a vision.

Clothing

Cheyenne clothing was designed for easy movement. In warm weather, most men wore only moccasins and breechcloths (material that goes between the legs and fastens at the waist). In colder weather, they also wore leggings and shirts. Women wore dresses and moccasins, and added leggings in winter. In the 16th and 17th centuries, clothes were usually made of deer or elk skins.

Everyday clothing was plain. Garments for ceremonial occasions could be very fancy, however. They might be decorated with beads, quillwork, bells, and fringes. Designs for men's clothing were determined by their standing as warriors. Often the

Northern Cheyenne men wore heavily beaded shirts.

Beadwork was used to decorate clothing and moccasins worn for special occasions.

A decorated shirt was worn during ceremonies or special events.

designs told a story about the person who wore them. The most spectacular garments were the knee-length shirts of warriors.

The Northern Cheyenne liked heavily beaded shirts. Southern Cheyenne shirts, on the other hand, had dark-green fringes, and relied on color for effect. Medicine bags, eagle feathers, and berry beads were also used for decoration. Men wore handsome robes when the weather was cold or to impress visitors.

Food

When the Cheyenne lived in Minnesota and the Dakotas, they raised corn, beans, and squash. They added deer and bear meat to the diet. When they moved to the Great Plains, Cheyenne men hunted

(left) Cheyenne women sometimes cooked meals in pots like this one.

(right) Women used fruit from the prickly pear cactus to thicken soups and stews.

buffalo. Women used all parts of the buffalo. They used the parts to make food, tepee coverings, and other items. Later, the Cheyenne traded with Americans for new kinds of foods. These included coffee, sugar, and flour.

Women cooked vegetables from their gardens. One of these vegetables was turnips, which were sliced, boiled, and dried in the sun. The women took fruit from the prickly pear cactus. This was difficult because the fruit had sharp spines. The dried fruit was used to thicken stews and soups. Women made balls from dried ground animal meat, dried berries, and animal fat. They also made another kind of ball with ground corn instead of meat.

Cheyenne girls learned how to care for children by watching their mothers tend babies.

Education

Cheyenne girls learned daily tasks as they watched their mothers and other women work. As they played with deerskin dolls, they imitated the way their mothers took care of babies. Boys learned to use small bows and arrows. They were taught to practice until they never missed a target. They also learned to hunt rabbits, turkeys, and fowl. Boys and girls were shown how to ride horses. Older boys were taught to tend the tribe's horses. When a boy reached the age of 12, his grandfather

A shaman performs a ritual.

Drums were an important part of Cheyenne healing rituals.

taught him about men's duties, such as buffalo hunts and horse raids.

Today, the Dull Knife Memorial College, a modern facility on the Northern Cheyenne Indian Reservation in southeastern Montana, serves 300 students. It offers associate degrees in arts and applied science. Programs also teach office skills and how to start a new business.

Healing practices

Cheyenne medicine men called shamans (pronounced SHAH-munz or SHAY-munz) performed healing rituals. They sucked the evil that caused illness out of a patient and spit it onto the ground. Shamans said prayers, blew whistles, and beat drums. They also used rattles made of gourds, animal bladders, or eagles' heads. Priests were called if the shamans failed to cure a patient. Priests wore more elaborate costumes and had more involved rituals than did shamans. They also performed minor surgery.

Drums were a key part of the healing process. The round shape of the drum represented the universe. Its steady beat was a symbol for the pulsing heart. Drums soothed troubled minds and healed bodies.

POPULATION OF CHEYENNE: 1990

There are four groups of Cheyenne in the United States. Their two major reservations are the Northern Cheyenne Reservation and the Cheyenne-Arapaho Reservation. The Northern Cheyenne Reservation covers nearly 450,000 acres in southeastern Montana. The Cheyenne-Arapaho Reservation spreads across an 8-county area in northwest and north-central Oklahoma. In the 1990 U.S. Census, members the various Cheyenne groups identified themselves this way:

Tribe	Population
Cheyenne	7,104
Northern Cheyenne	4,398
Southern Cheyenne	307
Cheyenne-Arapaho	2,629

SOURCE: "1990 census of population and housing. Subject summary tape file (SSTF) 13 (computer file): characteristics of American Indians by tribe and language." Washington, DC: U.S. Department of Commerce, Bureau of the Census, Data User Services division, 1995.

Cheyenne women were known for the way they decorated objects such as this beaded bag (left) and cradleboard (right).

Arts

Cheyenne women were known for the unique way they decorated objects. They used horsehair, feathers, and the bones and skin of animals. By the 1800s, they had begun to use items brought by white traders in their clothing and craft designs. Among these new types of decorations were trinkets, beads, paints, and metal.

Oral literature

The Cheyenne told war stories, sacred stories, and hero myths. An important figure was Wihio. He was a trickster who was similar to Coyote, a trickster found in the stories of many other tribes.

CUSTOMS

Festivals

The most sacred Cheyenne ceremony was the annual renewal of the Sacred Arrows. It took place at the summer solstice (when the sun is at its highest point at the tropic of Cancer). The Sacred Arrows had been found in the Black Hills of South Dakota by the prophet Sweet Medicine. He then brought them to the Cheyenne. The arrows' special powers helped the Cheyenne hunt buffalo and defeat their enemies in battle.

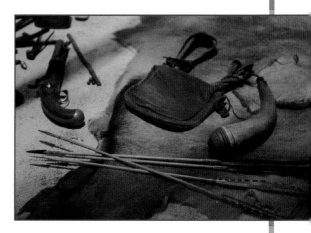

Arrows were used in the most important Cheyenne ceremony, the annual renewal of the Sacred Arrows.

Only men were allowed to attend the four-day ceremony. On the first day, offerings were brought to the Great Spirit. Men were chosen to build the Sacred Arrow Lodge. On the second day, a man was painted red and dressed only in a buffalo robe. He gave a bundle of sacred arrows to the high priest. The unity of each Cheyenne family within the tribe was celebrated on the third day. Sticks that represented each family were burned in an incense fire. On the fourth day, the sacred arrows were placed in the sunlight for the public to view. All the men and boys of the tribe walked past the arrows to take in their sacred powers. A large tepee called the Sweet Medicine Lodge was then set up over the arrows. That evening, the medicine men went inside the tepee and sang special songs. Just before dawn on the fifth day, all those involved went into the sweat lodge to be cleansed.

Today, several powwows and celebrations take place on the Northern Cheyenne Reservation in Montana. A powwow is a celebration that includes traditional songs and dances. In modern times, the singers and dancers come from many different tribes. In Oklahoma, the Cheyenne-Arapaho people hold three powwows each year. They are the Jackie Beard Pow Wow in May, the Cheyenne-Arapaho Summer Fest and Pow Wow in August, and the Veterans' Day Pow Wow in November.

Red Blanket, a Cheyenne warrior. Men belonged to one of five military societies.

War rituals

The Cheyenne had five military societies: Bowstring, Dog, Elk, Fox, and Shield. Four leaders were in charge of each society. Two were the war chiefs and decision-makers. The other two were peace leaders and representatives to other societies. Each group had its own war costumes, rituals, and chants. During the 1800s, the Dog Soldiers society fought with U.S. government troops. This society was the most famous and most feared on the Great Plains.

Courtship and marriage

A Cheyenne woman often waited years before she accepted a marriage proposal. A man never proposed to a woman directly. Instead, he asked an older female relative to take gifts to the woman's family and propose for him. If the woman accepted the proposal, the bride was brought to her husband's home. She was placed on a ceremonial blanket, carried into the tepee, and adorned with new clothes and paint. Then a feast was held. A very wealthy man might have several wives. If he did, he was expected to supply a tepee for each one.

Cheyenne women

Death

A close relative usually got a body ready for burial. The body was dressed in fine clothing and wrapped in blankets. It was then bound with ropes and carried to the burial site. Mourners sang and prayed. The deceased person's dearest possessions were placed next to the body. Other goods were given to non-relatives. A widow was allowed to keep only a blanket.

Current tribal issues

The use of the rich natural resources on their land is an important issue for the Cheyenne. In the late 1960s, coal was discovered on the reservation in

The efforts of the Cheyenne and other native groups led to a law that created the National Museum of the American Indian.

Montana. This gave the tribe a chance for economic independence. Supporters said that coal-mining income could help start education and health programs. These programs would make life on the reservation better. Others did not want to harm the environment. They thought coal companies would benefit, but the tribe would still be poor. In the end, the land was not mined.

Sacred sites and remains

In 1986, the Northern Cheyenne learned that the National Museum of American History in Washington, D.C., had the remains of thousands of deceased natives. It also held funeral objects (items that had been buried with the dead). Natives started a movement to win them back. Their work led to passage of the National Museum of the American Indian Act (1989) and the Native American Grave Protection and Reparations Act (1990).

The first act made the Smithsonian list all the remains and objects it held. It then had to give them back to the tribes. The act also allowed for a Native

American museum to be started. The second act required that local, state, or federal agencies also return any remains they held to their native tribes.

Notable people

Women's rights activist Suzan Shown Harjo (1945–) is a member of the Cheyenne and Arapaho tribes. She is a journalist and poet. She has worked in Washington, D.C., to change federal Indian policy.

Ben Nighthorse Campbell (1933–) is a member of the Northern Cheyenne tribe. In 1992, he became the first Native American elected to the U.S. Senate in more than 60 years. He is also the first Native American to lead the Senate Committee on Indian Affairs. He is of Apache-Pueblo-Cheyenne and Portuguese heritage. He has been a teacher, a horse breeder and trainer, and an award-winning jewelry designer and maker.

U.S. senators Ben Nighthorse Campbell (left) and Daniel Inouye attend the groundbreaking ceremony for the National Museum of the American Indian in Washington, D.C.

For More Information

Brown, Dee. "War Comes to the Cheyennes," in *Bury My Heart at Wounded Knee*. New York: Holt, 1970, pp. 67-102.

Hoig, Stan. *The Cheyenne.* New York: Chelsea House, 1989.

Lodge, Sally. *The Cheyenne.* Vero Beach, Florida: Rourke Publications, Inc., 1990.

Sneve, Virginia Driving Hawk. *The Cheyennes.* New York: Holiday House, 1996.

Sonneborn, Liz. *The Cheyenne Indians.* New York: Chelsea House Publishers, 1991.

Glossary

Ancestors dead relatives

Dwellings buildings

Reservation land set aside and given to Native Americans

Ritual something that is custom or done in a certain way

Sacred highly valued and important

Treaty agreement

Tribe a group of people who live together in a community

Index